James Sunney Quaicoe

The influences of selected socio-economic factors of parents and parenting attitudes on the academic achievements of their wards

Anchor Compact

Quaicoe, James Sunney: The influences of selected socio-economic factors of parents
and parenting attitudes on the academic achievements of their wards. Hamburg,
Anchor Academic Publishing 2014

Buch-ISBN: 978-3-95489-255-6
PDF-eBook-ISBN: 978-3-95489-755-1
Druck/Herstellung: Anchor Academic Publishing, Hamburg, 2014

Bibliografische Information der Deutschen Nationalbibliothek:
Die Deutsche Nationalbibliothek verzeichnet diese Publikation in der Deutschen
Nationalbibliografie; detaillierte bibliografische Daten sind im Internet über
http://dnb.d-nb.de abrufbar

Bibliographical Information of the German National Library:
The German National Library lists this publication in the German National Bibliography.
Detailed bibliographic data can be found at: http://dnb.d-nb.de

All rights reserved. This publication may not be reproduced, stored in a retrieval system
or transmitted, in any form or by any means, electronic, mechanical, photocopying,
recording or otherwise, without the prior permission of the publishers.

Das Werk einschließlich aller seiner Teile ist urheberrechtlich geschützt. Jede Verwertung
außerhalb der Grenzen des Urheberrechtsgesetzes ist ohne Zustimmung des Verlages
unzulässig und strafbar. Dies gilt insbesondere für Vervielfältigungen, Übersetzungen,
Mikroverfilmungen und die Einspeicherung und Bearbeitung in elektronischen Systemen.

Die Wiedergabe von Gebrauchsnamen, Handelsnamen, Warenbezeichnungen usw. in
diesem Werk berechtigt auch ohne besondere Kennzeichnung nicht zu der Annahme,
dass solche Namen im Sinne der Warenzeichen- und Markenschutz-Gesetzgebung als frei
zu betrachten wären und daher von jedermann benutzt werden dürften.

Die Informationen in diesem Werk wurden mit Sorgfalt erarbeitet. Dennoch können
Fehler nicht vollständig ausgeschlossen werden und die Diplomica Verlag GmbH, die
Autoren oder Übersetzer übernehmen keine juristische Verantwortung oder irgendeine
Haftung für evtl. verbliebene fehlerhafte Angaben und deren Folgen.

Alle Rechte vorbehalten

© Anchor Academic Publishing, ein Imprint der Diplomica® Verlag GmbH
http://www.diplom.de, Hamburg 2014
Printed in Germany

ABSTRACT

The purpose of the study was to explore the relation between selected Socio-economic and parenting factors on the academic performance of pupils. The study used a descriptive research designed type. A total of twenty-nine (29) pupils who are in Basic two were used for the study.

Questionnaires and test were the instruments used in gathering data on pupils and their parents. Responses from the pupils and their parents were treated statistically using frequency tables, percentages, mean, standard deviation and Pearson's Correlation as the tools.

Major findings from the study indicated that pupils' academic performance is just above average; and that the Socio- economic and parenting factors of the parents of the pupils' are also average. The study further established that there is a significant, medium and positive relation existing between the Socio-economic status of pupils' parents and pupils' academic performance; the parenting attitudes and pupils' academic performance. Finally, the study again established that there is a significant, medium relation between the Socio-economic status of pupils' parents and their parenting attitude or responsible parenting. Based the findings, suggestions in the form of recommendations were offered, which included; the need for deepened teacher – parent collaboration and the school undertaking activities to attract parents to the school.

ACKNOWLEDGEMENTS

This work would not have been possible without the help and support of some very important individuals and I am indeed indebted to the them. My supervisor – Joseph Tuffour Kwarteng - deserves my commendation for the courage and motivation he imbibed in me when he approved my proposal and subsequently moderating the entire exercise.

My spouse deserves a special mention for his support, encouragement and serving as time keeper to ensure that I meet all standards set for my assignments and this project – I am so grateful.

I am also grateful to all to all my course mates for their motivation - few of them deserve special commendation for the significant roles they played in making me enjoy this course and been such great friends and mothers.

My appreciation also goes the pupils of Archbishop Porter 'A' school, Effia Kuma for the joy and efficiency exhibited during the study. I equally thank the parents for their cooperation.

My final appreciation goes to members of staff of my school and members of my church for their various roles in motivating me to stand up to challenging moments and aspire to higher heights - I will forever be grateful to each one of you.

DEDICATION

To the Late Christina Pobee (*Maa*) and the Late Dorothy Ada Payne (*Mamaa*) may their souls rest in peace.

TABLE OF CONTENTS

ABSTRACT	1
ACKNOWLEDGEMENTS	2
DEDICATION	3
LIST OF TABLES	7

CHAPTER ONE:
INTRODUCTION 9

Background of the Study	9
Statement of the Problem	12
Purpose of the Study	14
Research	15
Significance of the Study	15
Delimitation	16
Limitations	17
Organisation of the study	18

CHAPTER TWO:
REVIEW OF RELATED LITERATURE 19

Introduction	19
Conceptual bases of parental roles, economic status and student academic achievement.	19
Empirical review on influence of parental variables on pupils' performance	21
Issues about education, parenting, socio-economic status and students' achievement	23
Conclusion	25

CHAPTER THREE:
METHODLOGY 27
Research design 27
Population 27
Sample and Sampling Technique 27
Instruments 28
Data Collection Procedure 28
Data Analysis Technique 29

CHAPTER FOUR:
RESULTS AND DISCUSSION 31
Background information 31
Academic performance of pupils 31
Socio-economic status of parents 32
Parenting attitude/responsibilities 38
Socio-economic status of parents and pupils' academic performance 44
Parenting attitudes and pupils' academic performance 45
Socio-economic status of parents and their parenting attitudes/responsibilities 46

CHAPTER FIVE:
SUMMARY, COCLUSION AND RECOMMENDATIONS 50
Summary 50
Conclusion 54
Recommendations 53
Suggestions for further research 53
REFERENCES 54
APPENDICES 56
A   Questionnaire 57
B   Pupils' Score 58

LIST OF TABLES

1. Statistics on the academic performance of pupils — 32
2. Highest qualification of one of parents — 33
3. Occupational status of one of your parents — 34
4. Position of the bread winner in his/her work place — 34
5. Estimated income of family at the end of the month — 35
6. Families with car — 35
7. Families with Television — 36
8. Families with fridge — 36
9. Parents holding Religious positions — 37
10. Families affording three meals a day — 37
11. Families with siblings attaining tertiary education — 38
12. Overall Socio-economic status of parents — 38
13. Overall results of parental attitude/ responsibilities to pupils — 39
14. Descriptive Statistics parenting attitude/level of responsibility — 41
15. Relation between socio-economic status of parents and pupils' academic performance — 44
16. Relation between parenting attitude and pupils' academic performance — 36
17. Relation between socio-economic status of parents and parenting attitude — 45

CHAPTER ONE

INTRODUCTION

Background of the study

An individual's educational achievements is closely linked to numerous factors for which some may be known and others not. Battle and Lewis (2002), share the view that one's life chances, income and his/her overall well being is determined by his/her education. Education is therefore viewed as the medium through which mankind gains a full capacity of his/her potentialities – through integrated activities such as teaching, learning, assessment, remedial activities and classification of pupils' achievement levels for placement and/or decision making. Consequently, the significance of education in the overall development of children cannot be overemphasised.

In Ghana, the education of children of all school going age can be said to be a national priority. This is evidenced in the implementation of the Free Compulsory Basic Education (fCUBE) policy. Practically, governments- both past and present - have displayed commitment to the implementation of this policy in the form of "creating opportunities and strengths in primary education" (Mankoe 2001:12). Some of the opportunities in primary school education include; payment of capitation grant of GHc 4.50 per pupil per year(GHc 1.50 per term), provision of free meals, provision of teachers, provision of free textbooks and in some cases exercise books and syllabuses – including other teaching learning materials and support for pupils. All these injections are virtually free and aimed at alleviating if not completely to the barest minimum the financial obligations of parents on the basic education of their wards. This comes with the assumption that parents have very little financial obligations when it comes to their wards primary education.

Many researchers (Barry 2005; Crosnoe, Jonhson & Elder 2004) in their works have identified that the academic achievement of children in school have links with the Socio-economic status (SES) of their parents. Some of these socio-economic variables used by Barry for the study included the following; sex, race, family backgrounds, neighbourhood, parents' educational attainment, nature of work and family incomes, among other things. Majoribanks, (1996), have observed that there are direct links between family backgrounds and the achievement of pupils.

Conditions at the home of children or pupils basically constitute the fundamental social agent influencing the interest aspirations and performances. Linking this assertion to that of the study conducted by Jeynes (2002), it has been established that the SES of parents and the extent of their responsible parenting influence the academic performance of their children in the school and in their engagement in extracurricular activities of these as well .

Researchers have concluded that economic hardships that arise in families and which eventually either motivates or derail the learning attitudes of children have their roots in the SES of parents (Baharudin and Luster, 1998; Jeynes, 2002; Majoribanks, 1999; Eamon, 2005). In each of the literature cited their conclusions point to the fact that SES of parents do influence the total development of their wards to a large extent. That the effects of the SES of parents predisposes the pupils to conditions that may either enhance or derail their learning and schooling attitudes.

The SES of parents has been described by Ainley et al, (1995) as a parent's overall social and economic position as a result of his/her education, kind of profession, income levels and wealth - among other indicators that go to establish his/her social and financial independence or self reliance.

Literature reviewed gives the implication that the SES of parents do not only influence the learning habitats of their wards, but also spill over to determine the kind of parenting they offer to their children. This latter assertion is made in the context of the level of interest shown by parents in the educational activities and issues of their wards. The resultant outcome of the combination of the SES of parents and the kind of parenting they offer their children in no doubt go a long way to determine the academic achievements of their children (Baharudin and Luster, 1998; Jeynes, 2002; Majoribanks, 1999; Eamon, 2005; Ainley et al, 1995). That parents with low SES tend to have their children performing below the required standard of achievement, whiles children of parents with high SES may perform either up to the standard achievement levels or even beyond. In each of the cases illustrated above, SES of parents has been identified to have a bearing on the kind of parenting attitudes exhibited towards their wards – with the resultant being that their wards may either meet the academic and educational standards confronting him/her or miss out.

Notwithstanding, the research findings (Baharudin and Luster, 1998; Jeynes, 2002; Majoribanks, 1999; Eamon, 2005; Ainley et al, 1995) do not constitute a predictive indicators operating as definite yardsticks for the well being and academic achievements of pupils in the Archbishop Porter Primary School in Effia Kuma in the Sekondi Takoradi Metropolis. The reasons being that children from low SES parents who happen to receive the right parenting attitude and support for teachers could do well in their academic performances in school; whiles as a pupil a from parent with high SES who may encounter a non supportive school conditions – either from parents, or class teacher or both may not do well in his/her academic pursuits.

It is therefore a worthwhile venture for teachers and the academia to undertake various academic exercises capable of bringing to the fore empirical facts on the subject-matter under discussion in a customised manner. Through this teachers will be better and professionally placed to offer learners the relevant support towards their academic pursuits and further map out schemes to enhance effective collaboration with parents for the welfare of their wards. It is in this light, that this study is being initiated to specifically investigate primary school pupils in the context of how selected parental based factors influence their academic performances in school.

Statement of Problem

Governments' commitment and support in the direction of providing Free Compulsory Basic Education to all Ghanaian children have been massive over the years. This is evidenced in the provision of funding and materials to children free of charge. Parents therefore do not have excuse when it comes to access to education for their wards. Financial constraint as an inhibitor to primary education can no longer be considered a key factor. The reason being that Capitation Grants is paid to run the schools; pupils are fed on free meals during school and free school uniforms and exercise books are occasionally given to pupils free of charge. In addition, textbooks and teaching learning materials are supplied by the Ministry of Education through the Ghana Education Service.

These interventions therefore seem to suggest that greater percentages of the financial burdens of parents who have their wards in the Archbishop Porter "A" School are lessened dramatically. It is therefore assumed that the key responsibility of parents therefore is to show much interest in the school activities and learning of their wards – by way of good parenting.

Presently, the general outcry amongst teachers at the Archbishop Porter Primary School is that parents are not supportive when it comes to the learning of their wards; as a result the children are not performing well academically. However, there is no definite evidence to this assertion, no literature exist that empirically accounts for the relation between the performance of pupils and the attitude of parents with specific reference to the primary school children in Archbishop Porter "A" School at Effia Kuma.

The problem therefore is that with the numerous interventions made by governments to make primary education free over the years, is there still a relation between the SES of parents and the academic achievements of their wards; and what kind of parenting is being received by the pupils of Archbishop Porter Primary School; and to what extent are the two variables named influencing the academic achievements of the pupil. In an attempt to find answers to these enquiries this study was initiated, so as to find out the extent to which SES of parents and the parenting attitudes influences pupils' academic achievement.

Purpose of the study

The general objective of the study is to establish the relation between a parents' SES, parenting attitudes and the academic achievement of their wards. In a more detail form the specific objectives of the study was as follows;

1. To identify the level of academic achievement of pupils in the subjects areas studied regularly in school,
2. To find the SES of parents based on some selected factors,
3. To find the extent to which parents are offering responsible parenting to their wards,
4. To find the relation between the SES of parents and the academic achievement of their wards,
5. To find the relation parenting attitudes and the academic achievement of their wards,
6. Establish the relation between the SES of parents and their parenting attitudes.

Research Questions

The study was guided by the following research questions;

1. What are the levels of academic achievement of pupils in Archbishop Porter "A" Primary School?
2. What is the SES of parents of the pupils in Archbishop Porter "A" Primary School?
3. To what extent are parents supporting the school activities of their wards in the form of responsible parenting?
4. Is there any statistical relation between the SES of parents and the academic achievements of pupils?
5. Is there any statistical relation between parenting attitudes and the academic achievement of the pupil?
6. Is there a statistical relation between the SES of parents and the kind of parenting they offer to their wards education?

Significance of the Study

Every research work potentially have the capacity to unravel new knowledge or better still describe a prevailing situation and further attempt to suggest possible interventions or recommendation. The significance of this study therefore lies in its ability to satisfy the above named assertions within the school system in the Sekondi Takoradi Metropolis. On a more specific note, the study will be useful to parents, class teachers, head teachers and circuit supervisors in the form of providing information on factors influencing the academic achievements of pupils in the schools.

Again, the study has the potential to inform school authorities; SMCs and PTA of the school on the SES of parents and their parenting attitudes; and how it is affecting the general profile of the school's activities and their wards; and how the situation could be addressed in favour of the pupils.

The documented report of the findings of the study will be a reference material in the educational circles – precisely offer new and additional knowledge in research and development on educational issues in the Sekondi Takoradi Metropolis.

Finally, the study has the capacity to inform teachers on the needs an challenges facing their pupils and resultantly guide them to effectively their needs professionally.

Delimitation of the study

The study was delimited to Archbishop Porter Primary School at Effia Kuma in the Sekondi Takoradi Metropolis; and further restricted to the primary school. The study did not cover upper primary pupils and students at the Junior High School level.

It took the form of a case study of pupils in a sampled class and the scope will be as follows; established the SES of their parents, explored the kind of concern parents' show to their wards' education in the form of their parenting attitudes and established the academic achievement of the pupils. The study established the correlation between the named parental variables and the academic achievements of pupils.

The scope for the measuring of the pupils' achievement will be on the six subjects studied by primary school pupils, namely; Mathematics, Language and Literacy, Natural Science, Information Communication Technology, Religious and Moral Education and Creative Arts.

The study will not attempt to predict the future performance of the pupils, but basically relate the parental attitudes and SES to the academic performance of their wards by way of computing the statistical relations among the variables.

Limitations of the Study

Due to time and financial constraints the study was restricted to the Sekondi Takoradi Metropolis and precisely to the Effia Tanokrom Circuit. These limitations raises reliability and validity questions .To ensure the validity and the reliability of the study the following steps were taken in the course of the study, (a) questionnaires and items therein were derived from the literature review so as to measure what the study indented to investigate – in this case explore the SES of parents, their parenting styles and the academic performance of their wards, (b) the sampled class had all its members participating in the study to give the room for generalization of the findings, (c) the main subjects of the study were given ample time to give their responses and again their anxiety about the exercise were allayed with the assurance that they were part of an academic exercise and not under investigation and that their responses will be treated confidential.

Finally, the internal consistency of the instruments was tested using Cronbach's Alpha Coefficient. The results were as follow;, 39 item questionnaire ($\alpha = .91$) and the 18 test results ($\alpha = .94$).

Organisation of the Study

The report of the study is organised into five chapters, followed by references and appendices. The first chapter is the introduction and contains the background information, statement of problems, research questions, the purpose and significance of the study. Information on limitations and delimitations of the study is also catered for in this chapter. Organisation of the study as a sub-topic closes the entire chapter.

The second chapter is titled literature review and looks into concepts, research findings and publications relevant to issues on Socio-economic status, parenting and student performance. It is followed by Chapter Three which outlines the methods that were used for the study. It describes the research design type used, population and the sample for the study; instruments used and procedures for data collection; and then ends with the methods used for analysing collected data.

Chapter Four is titled as results and discussions and comes after chapter three. It covers the results or findings of the study together with their corresponding discussions. It offers medium for inferences to be made by virtue of responses gathered from the participants of the research. This chapter is immediately followed by Chapter Five which contains the summary, conclusions and recommendations of the study. References and appendices are provided at the back of the report and that close the entire document.

CHAPTER TWO

REVIEW OF RELATED LITERATURE

This chapter delves into written materials, papers and works of individuals and authorities in the field of Socio-economic studies, social studies and sociology, educational assessment and evaluation The content is arranged under the following sub headings;

1. Conceptual bases of parental roles and economic status and student academic achievement.
2. Empirical review – Socio-economic Status of Parents, and Student Performance
3. Issues about parenting styles and socio-economic status

Conceptual bases of parental roles, economic status and student academic achievement.

The growth and development of every society is likened to her children who are considered as the future generation and leaders. Apparently, the growth and development of these futures is influenced by various factors including the home, community, parents, and friends among other factors. The home and that much parents however, have greater influence on the total development of the children.

During the era of Traditional Education in Ghana the subject of child's development, training and upbringing was a shared responsibility of immediate family members, extended family members and the community. Parents therefore, had the opportunity to get feedback on the performance of their wards. Again with the traditional approach to child development, assessment and performance the conduct of the child, parental expected parental standards and responsibility are visible to members of the community to determine how responsible parents and relative are or how bad or delinquent the child is. Therefore, in order to avoid disgrace as a result of the acts of their children parents went all out to ensure that their children excel in all trainings given at home and in the society – for the success and achievement of their wards bring to them honour and respect to them.

The contrast however, is that in this modern era, parents are adopting the nuclear family structure which implies that children have their parents as their key mentors. Thus the kind of things that children see their parent do is what they will emulate, the extent of parental expectation will drive their wards' achievement and finally, the kind of parenting and level of self-reliance of parents will influence the total upbringing of the child.

By and large, it is apparent that reasoning in the context of modern child up bring, parents will have to send their children to school to be trained and it is expected that parents will give their wards every support that will aid their wards to be achievers. It is therefore worth noting that the success of children in the school today, just like in the traditional system of education is influenced by parental influences, attitudes and behaviour of the parents.

The academia have given this subject extensive attention with hope that by gaining in depth understanding of issue the child in today's educational institutions would be understood better and appropriately helped to an achiever in her/her academic pursuits. These conceptual bases is underpinning this study which has to do with localising the study to obtain facts on parenting attitudes, their socio-economic status and how these factor impact upon the academic achievement of pupils in the Effia Kuma community.

Empirical review on influence of parental variables on pupils' performance.

Various researchers have conducted extensive studies on the performance or the academic achievement of children in school, and in all the studies reviewed to main categories with their respective variables have been identified. These two main classifications are the home conditions and school conditions. In line with this assertion, Considine and Zappala (n.d) hold the view that there is a relationship between a families' Socio-economic Status (SES) and the academic performances of pupils. This assertion resulted from a study conducted to identify factors influencing the performance of students from disadvantaged backgrounds. Their findings indicated that low SES of parents adversely affects the educational outcomes of their wards.

In another study carried out in Pakistan by Hajazi and Naqvi (2006) they sought to identify factors affecting student performance. The study revealed that aside other factor, parents' level of income, mother's education and age constitute factors influencing their wards' performance.

On the part of Walberg (1984) he asserts that an academically stimulated home is a key determinant of learning behaviours of students. This assertion is derived from a study carried out to establish the relationship between the SES of parents and the academic performance of their wards.

In a similar study carried out by Walters (1998) it was found out that student performance is very much dependent of SES backgrounds of parents,

Reynolds et al (1993) however concluded in their studies that the most constant predictor of children's academic achievement and social adjustment were linked to the expectations of their parents, parents' educational attainment and extent of parental satisfaction with their wards' education at a school. Again, Davis-Kean (1999) conducted a study on the effect of Socio-economic characteristics on parenting and child outcome, and concluded that responsible parenting plays a significant role in the academic achievement of students. It was further established in that study Socio-economic factors are directly linked to the academic achievement of school children.

In a more recent studies conducted by (Hanafi, 2008; Barry 2005; Crosnoe, Jonhson and Elder 2004) , it was established that factors influencing academic success in children include SES of parents and parenting styles.

In conclusion, Henderson (1994) established in his works that families whose children are doing well in school exhibits similar characteristics and these included;

1. Possess established family routine,
2. Monitor out of school activities of their children,
3. Served as models for their children in the context learning, hard work and self-discipline,
4. Express high but realistic expectations for their wards achievement,
5. Encourage children's development and progress in school,
6. Encourage family interactions through discussions, reading and writing.

Issues about education, parenting, socio-economic status and students' achievement

The significance of education in the overall development of children cannot be overemphasised, in the view of Battle and Lewis (2002), one's life chances, income and his/her overall well being is determined by his/her education. Education is therefore viewed as the medium through which mankind gains a full capacity of his/her potentialities – through integrated activities such as teaching, learning, assessment, remedial activities and classification of pupils' achievement levels for placement and/or decision making.

. Many researchers including (Barry 2005; Crosnoe, Jonhson and Elder 2004) identified that the academic achievement of children in school is influenced by various factors. In his study Barry used ; sex, race, family backgrounds, neighbourhood, parents' educational attainment, nature of work and family incomes, as independent variables impacting on student performace.

The argument therefore, stands that the home of children or pupils basically constitute the fundamental social agent influencing the interest aspirations and performances. Linking this assertion to that of the study conducted by Jeynes (2002), it has been established that the SES of parents and the extent of their responsible parenting influence the academic performance of their children in the school and in their engagement in extracurricular activities of these as well .

Researchers have concluded that economic hardships that arise in families and which eventually either motivates or derail the learning attitudes of children have their roots in the SES of parents (Baharudin and Luster, 1998; Jeynes, 2002; Majoribanks, 1999; Eamon, 2005).

The SES of parents has been described by Ainley et al, (1995) as a parent's overall social and economic position as a result of his/her education, kind of profession, income levels and wealth - among other indicators that go to establish his/her social and financial independence or self reliance.

Literature reviewed gives the implication that the SES of parents do not only influence the learning habitats of their wards, but also spill over to determine the kind of parenting they offer to their children. This latter assertion is made in the context of the level of interest shown by parents in the educational activities and issues of their wards. The resultant outcome of the combination of the SES of parents and the kind of parenting they offer their children in no doubt go a long way to determine the academic achievements of their children (Baharudin and Luster, 1998; Jeynes, 2002; Majoribanks, 1999; Eamon, 2005; Ainley et al, 1995). That parents with low SES tend to have their children performing below the required standard of achievement, whiles children of parents with high SES may perform either up to the standard achievement levels or even beyond. In each of the cases illustrated above, SES of parents has been identified to have a bearing on the kind of parenting attitudes exhibited towards their wards – with the resultant being that their wards may either meet the academic and educational standards confronting him/her or miss out.

Notwithstanding, the research findings (Baharudin and Luster, 1998; Jeynes, 2002; Majoribanks, 1999; Eamon, 2005; Ainley et al, 1995) do not constitute a predictive indicators operating as definite yardsticks for the well being and academic achievements of every pupil in the schooling system. This point is supported by Okafor (2007) who share a counter view that SES of parents and their parenting styles are the determinants of the performance of their wards. He argues that their equal empirical bases asserting that despite the threat of low SES families having their wards performing poorly in school, others in the same level of SES have recorded remarkable academic success in their academic pursuits

The arguments advanced by Okafor therefore, brings to the fore the fact that determining the factors influencing student performance is an arduous one. That measuring student performance cannot be restricted to the physical and observable variables alone, but the cognitive level of the child, personality of pupils and all environmental influences having the capacity to impact on the child's learning should be investigated as well.

Nonetheless, the literature review up to this point summarises the entire issues raised that some factors influence the academic performance of school going children, and that if parents will offer responsible parenting and meet the basic needs of their wards such as food, shelter, clothing and care the children will be motivated enough to be achievers in their own right.

Conclusion

The relevant literature reviewed sofa points to the fact the education play a significant role in determining the overall well being of individuals. Assessment and evaluation of student performance forms part of the procedure to measure the learning outcomes of the student.

These student learning outcomes are influenced by number of factors. Researchers cited listed SES, parenting attitude and styles, performance of students/pupils. There is however a counter view that determining student performance is not that easy and simply and that SES and parenting attitudes alone cannot holistically determine the academic achievements of pupils. Other factors such as such as cognitive level of children, their personality and the learning environment are additional factors that impact on the learning outcomes of pupils.

Notwithstanding, no matter which direction the pendulum would swing to one thing stood out clear that the extent of care in the context of love and affection, provision of basic needs of the children and showing interest in the well being of the child will invariably motivate the child to be responsible and achieve all endeavours of which he/she is involved, including academic achievements and personality development.

CHAPTER THREE

METHODOLOGY

Research Design

The study adopted a Descriptive Research design approach and used the survey technique. These approaches were deemed appropriate to the investigator on the bases that the fundamental objective of the study is to describe a relation between variables and not to manipulate the variables to obtain results. Furthermore, the study is not an experiment research design, and consequently no variables are going to be controlled.

In addition to the above made points, the selection of this technique was influenced by the investigators familiarity and comprehension of principles and procedures surrounding the use of this research design type.

Population

Archbishop Porter Primary School is a four-stream school grouped into two main schools namely "Porter A1" and "Porter A2". The population for the study will be the pupils in the lower primary classes. A total 216 pupils are enrolled in the lower classes – these therefore constitute the population for the study.

Sample and Sampling Technique

A purposive sampling technique was adopted to select the participating class used for the study. This technique was selected due to its capacity to target the actual class for the study and further offer opportunity to the investigator to obtain information from pupils who are well known by the her and further aid the participants to have their fears allayed throughout the study. Thus, creating a rapport that will enable participants' to devolve family information voluntarily on the bases that they are acquainted with the researcher. The census approach was used on the sampled class. In all twenty-nine pupils (29) took part in the study.

Instruments

Questionnaire and Test (Examination Results) were used as instruments for data collection. Close-ended questionnaire was used to measure the SES of parents and their parenting attitudes, whiles the Test patterned on School Based Assessment (SBA) approach was used to obtain information on the academic achievements of the pupils.

These instruments were selected based on their capacity to measure the intend variables, namely SES of parents and their parenting attitudes; and the performance of pupils.

Data collection procedure

The pupils in the sampled class and their parents were the source for data collection for the study. A Questionnaire containing 21 items was administered on participants to obtain data on parenting attitude and the SES of their parents. Due to their ages and their level of reasoning, the investigator guided them closely as they related to their parents in order to respond to all items on the questionnaire. The exercise was carried out in phases and stretched throughout the academic year so that the data collection exercise was patterned to serve as project work to the pupils.

Test results of pupils on six subject areas served as data for determining the academic performances of the participants. The subjects were Mathematic, Natural Science, Language and Literacy, Information Communication Technology and Religious and Moral Education. The results of three terms were used; they constituted two terms of previous academic work and one term results of present class performance.

Data Analysis

The study investigated three main variables namely, the academic performances of the participants, the SES of their parents and the parenting attitudes. The academic performance of the participants was measured with an ordinal scale structured to display merit rating of their achievement levels. This was adopted from the grading system of Ghana Education Service for basic schools, which is a six- point scale ranging from Excellent to Fail. The overall academic performance measure was then transformed into a four-point scale how far their performances are from the average. The statistical tools used for the analysis were the frequency table, mean and standard deviation.

The SES of parents was measured using nominal scales to establish the status or categories parents fall under. Percentages and frequency distributions were the statistical tools used for the data analysis.

The variable measuring parenting attitudes was measured with a continuous scale, precisely a three-point Likert Scale to measure the extent to which parents are being responsible to the educational issues of their wards in the school. The statistical tools for the analysis were the mean and standard deviations.

The overall analysis the study sought to establish the relations between the three main variables for the study, based on that SPSS version 18 was used in determine the Coefficient of Correlation of the variables, and also used to compute the mean, standard deviations and percentages of the data obtained.

The treated data were presented on tables for discussion and making inferences.

CHAPTER FOUR

RESULTS AND DISCUSSION

Background information

The data collection activities took one term, which is three months to complete. The study had as it aim to investigate the impact of parental attitudes and SES on the performance of pupils in Archbishop Porter 'A'School at Effia Kuma in the Sekondi Takoradi Metropolis. In all 19 girls and 10 boys, totalling 29 pupils took part in the study. The study recorded 100% participation of all pupils in the class.

Questionnaire and Test were the instruments used for the study. The questionnaire was used to elicit parental information, while the test measured student academic performance in the six subjects studied at the lower primary. Both nominal and ordinal scales were used in measuring respective variables and eventually taken through statistical analysis using SPSS Version 18. The treated data is presented in tables and under respective research questions for discussion.

Academic performance of pupils

Research question one was on the academic performance of the pupils. A six-point scale ranging from excellent to fail was used the measure the level of students performance. All the six subjects mandated by the Ghana Education Service for lower primary classes were used in establishing the performance of the pupils. Tables 1 displays the information on the performance of the pupils in Mathematic, Language and literacy, Creative arts, Natural science, Religious and moral education and Information communication technology.

Table 1:

Statistics on the academic performance of pupils

Subjects	No. of pupils	Mean	Standard Deviation	Minimum	Maximum
Language and Literacy	29	13.3	3.4	6	18
Mathematics	29	14.6	3.0	8	18
ICT	29	12.0	2.8	8	16
Natural Science	29	13.1	3.6	5	18
Creative Arts	29	13.3	2.6	9	17
R.M.E.	29	12.8	3.1	8	18
Overall Performance	29	2.5	1.2	1	4

From Table 7 the overall performance of pupils just above average (M = 2.5, SD = 1.2) on a four point scale. However in a detail respective subject performance standings the following is shown; Language and literacy just above average (M = 13.3, SD = 3.4), Mathematics, just above average (M = 14.6, SD = 3.0), ICT, average (M = 12.0, SD = 2.8), Natural Science, just above average (M = 13.1, SD = 3.6), Creative Arts, just above average (M = 13.3, SD = 2.6) and RME, just below average (M = 12.8, SD = 3.1).

Socio-economic status of parents

Research question two was on the Socio-economic status of parent based on selected SES indicators. A nominal scale was used in measuring this variable.

Responses elicited from the parents are presented on Tables 2 to 11 shows selected SES of parents.

Table 2:

Highest level of qualification of one of the parents/guardian.

Items	Frequency	Percent (%)
Elementary/Primary School	6	20.7
JHS/Middle School	11	37.9
Vocational Training	1	3.4
SHS/Technical Institute	6	20.7
University/Degree	2	6.9
Postgraduate	3	10.3
Total	29	100.0

Table 2 shows that only 5 parents out of the 29 participants have university education, constituting 17.2%, while 20.7% have attained elementary education, 37.9% have middle school/Junior High School Education. A total 7 parents have attained some form second cycle education in the form of 20.7% attend Senior High school or Technical School and 3.4% attending a vocational school.

Table 3:

Occupational status of one of your parents

Items	Frequency	Percent
Casual/Part time work	2	6.9
Engaged in full time work	13	44.8
Run his/her own business	14	48.3
Total	29	100.0

Table 3 shows that 6.9% of the parents of the pupils are not engaged in full time jobs, 44.8% are engaged in full time jobs. A total of 14 parents representing 48.3% run their own enterprises.

Table 4:

Position of the bread winner in his/her work place

Items	Frequency	Percent
Labourer	1	3.4
Skilled/Artisan	4	13.8
Headman/Foreman	4	13.8
Supervisor	6	20.7
Manager/Director	14	48.3
Total	29	100.0

Out of the 29 pupils, Table 4 shows that 3.4% of the parents work labourers, 13.8% are skilled artisans, 13.8% function in their work places as either headmen or foremen. At the top position level 20.7% of the parents are found to be supervisors, while 48.3% are managers or directors in their business or at the work place.

Table 5:

Estimated income of family at the end of the month

Income Levels	Frequency	Percent
Between GHc 50.00 - GHc 150.00	5	17.2
Between GHc 150.00 - GHc 500.00	11	37.9
Between 500 .00 -GHc1000	13	44.8
Total	29	100.0

Table 5 shows that 17.2% of parents peg their monthly income between GHc50.00 to GHc150, 37.9% indicated that their monthly income available in a month is from GHc 150.00 to GHc500.00, while 44.8% indicated an income of GHc 500.00 and above.

Table 6:

Families with car

Responses	Frequency	Percent
No	14	48.3
Yes	15	51.7
Total	29	100.0

From Table 6 48.3 of parents responded that they have no cars, while 51.7% indicated that they do have cars at their disposal.

Table 7:

Families with Television

Responses	Frequency	Percent
No	3	10.3
Yes	26	89.7
Total	29	100.0

A total of 89.7% of families used for the study indicated that they have televisions in their home, while only 10.3% indicated that they do not have television in their homes.

Table 8:

Families with fridge

Responses	Frequency	Percent
No	9	31.0
Yes	20	69.0
Total	29	100.0

Table 8 shows that 69% of families have fridge, while 31% do not have the gadget in their homes.

Table 9:

Parents holding Religious positions

Responses	Frequency	Percent
No	7	24.1
Yes	22	75.9
Total	29	100.0

Table 9 shows that 75.9% of the parents show religious commitments as leaders, while 24.1% have no religious leadership commitments.

Table 10:

Families affording three meals a day

Responses	Frequency	Percent
No	7	24.1
Yes	22	75.9
Total	29	100.0

Table 10 shows majority of the families (75.6%) can afford three square meals; while 24.1% of families are not able afford three meals a day.

Table 11:

Families with siblings attaining tertiary education

Responses	Frequency	Percent
No	7	24.1
Yes	22	75.9
Total	29	100.0

Table 11 shows that most of the pupils (75.9%) have siblings having had tertiary education; whiles 24.1% have no member of their family having had tertiary education.

Table 12:

Overall Socio-economic status of parents

	Frequency	Percent
Low SES	4	13.8
Average SES	12	41.4
High SES	13	44.8
Total	29	100.0

From Table 12 only 13.8% of families have Low SES, 41.4% have Average SES and 44.8% were found to have High SES.

Parenting attitude/responsibilities

Research question three was on the parenting attitude of parent based on selected indicators depicting the extent to which they are supporting wards' education. An ordinal nominal scale was used in measuring this variable. Responses elicited from the parents are presented on Tables 13 and 14.

Table 13 gives the overall level of parental responsibility to their wards per predetermined indicators (See appendix A). The analysis is scaled under three

Table 13:

Overall results of parental attitude/ responsibilities to pupils

Level of Parental Responsibility(Attitude)	Frequency	Percent (%)
Not at all	11	37.9
Sometimes	15	51.7
Always	3	10.3
Total	29	100.0

Table 13 summarizes that 37.9% of parents showed signs of not been responsible at all, while 51.7% are sometimes responsible. Only 10.3% fell within the scale of always being responsible.

Further analysis using descriptive statistical tool is shown on Table 14. Shows that the overall level of parental responsibility or attitude to their wards education far above average (M = 2.1, SD = .71). This has some bearing on the results on Table13, which indicate that only 37.9% displayed irresponsible parenting

Notwithstanding, in some areas (variables) parental attitude towards the wards' education was very disappointing, these include; parents monitoring the regularity and punctuality of their wards in their schools (M = 1.3, SD = .55), parents visiting to the school to look at exercise and observe their what is their books (M = 1.4, SD = .68), accompany children to school(M = 1.5, SD = .63).

Table 14:

Descriptive Statistics parenting attitude/level of responsibility

Items	N	Min	Max	Mean	Std. Deviation
I attend PTA meetings	29	1	3	1.9	.57
I visit my child at his/her school to check his/her regularity and punctuality at school.	29	1	3	1.3	.55
I visit my child's school to observe his work/exercises.	29	1	3	1.4	.68
I inspect the home work my child brings from school.	29	1	3	2.1	.62
I assist my child to ensure home work is done.	29	1	3	2.3	.70
I read my child's end of term assessment report (Report Card).	29	2	3	2.7	.47
I interview and counsel child about school life.	29	1	3	2.3	.75
I attend funfair and merry making occasions with my child. (E.g. Beach, Party etc).	29	1	3	1.8	.66
I attend church/mosque/religious ceremonies with child.	29	1	3	2.3	.65
I accompany my child to school.	29	1	3	1.5	.63
I ensure that my child studies after school before he/she goes to sleep.	29	1	3	2.2	.80
Total (Overall Rating)	**29**	1	3	2.1	.71

Most parents however, displayed responsible parenting in the following areas (variables), inspect wards' home work (M = 2.1, SD = .68), ensure that wards' home work is done (M = 2.3, SD =.70), read wards' end of term reports (M =

2.7, SD = .47), Counsel and interview ward on school issues (M = 2.3, SD = .75) and ensuring ward study before going to bed (M = 2.2, SD =.80)

The perception of teachers at the Archbishop Porter 'A' School is that the parents of their pupils are not being responsible and complain of economic hardships and these conditions are affecting the academic performances of the pupils. This premise is equally held by the academia that the level of parental responsibility and their SES have some influence on the academic performance of pupils (Barry 2005; Crosnoe, Jonhson and Elder 2004).

Since the view of the teachers are speculative by nature, there was the need to appeal for empirical confirmation, data gathered and analysed however portray a contradicting picture from that of the teachers in the dimensions of 1) the academic performance of the pupils, 2) the SES of the parents of the pupils and finally the extent of responsible parent being offered to the pupils by their parents.

From Table 1 it is established that pupils in Archbishop Porter School having an average age of seven years are not under achievers in their academic performance. In each of the six subject areas in which the pupils were evaluated they proved to be either average or above average. And in the overall analysis the class average for the entire six subject as found on Table 1 stood as above average (M = 2.5, SD = 1.2) on a four point scale.

Again, information gathered on the Socio-economic status is shown on Table 12. On the table 44.8% of parents of the pupils displayed high level of SES, while 41.4% found themselves in the category of have average SES.

Only 13.8% recorded low SES. These findings further go to disabuse the view points of the teachers as depicted from Table 2 to Table 11.

Finally, investigation on the kind of parenting being offered to these young yielded interesting results ad depicted on Table 13. From Table 13, it is established that only 40% parents fell under the category irresponsible parenting, while 51.9% of the parents fell under the category of being sometimes responsible, however 10.3% of the parents had the highest rating of being always responsible. Further analysis as shown on Table 14 indicates that in the overall analysis of the parenting attitude or the extent responsible parenting given to their wards are above average(M =2.1, SD = .71).

Referring to Tables 14 there are however, some areas parents failed woefully, these include; parents monitoring the regularity and punctuality of their wards in their schools (M = 1.3, SD = .55), parents visiting to the school to look at exercise and observe their what is their books (M = 1.4, SD = .68), accompany children to school(M = 1.5, SD = .63).

In conclusion, pupils in Archbishop 'A' school with an average age of 7 years and having a class average of 2.5 and Standard Deviation of 1.2 on a four point scale cannot be described as performing poorly academically. Again, a look at the SES of their parent and the extent of parenting attitudes give cause for further discussions on the subject at stake. This assertion is based on the fact the shortfalls in the SES as indicated on Table 2 is being intervened by the School feeding scheme and the provision of capitation grants that reduces the burden of parents from the low SES. It is therefore worth subjecting this discussion to the establishing the statistical relations between the variables.

Socio-economic status of parents and pupils' academic performance

Research question four was on finding the statistical relationship between SES of the parents and pupils' academic performance since both variables were transformed into continuous scales, Pearson Product Moment Correlation Coefficient was used for the analysis. Table 15 contains information on the relationship between two variables.

Table 15

Relation between socio-economic status of parents and pupils' academic performance

		Socio-economic Status of parents
Pupils' Performance	Pearson Correlation	.463*
	Sig. (2-tailed)	.011
	N	29

*. Correlation is significant at the 0.05 level (2-tailed).

Table 15 shows that there is a significant relation between pupils' performance and the SES of their parents, but has a medium and positive correlation between them ($r(29) = .463$, $p < 0.05$). The implication this findings gives is that the two variables tend to change in the same direction, and in the context of our investigation, increase in the SES of parents of the pupils, will yield an increase in the performances of the pupils, on the other hand decrease in the SES of the parents will have a corresponding low performance of the pupils.

Parenting attitudes and pupils' academic performance

Research question five was on finding the statistical relationship between parenting attitude/responsibilities and pupils' academic performance; again since both variables were transformed into continuous scales, Pearson Product Moment Correlation Coefficient was used for the analysis. Table 16 contains information on the relationship between two variables.

Table 16

Relation between parenting attitude and pupils' academic performance

		Parenting Attitude/Responsibility
Pupils' Performance	Pearson Correlation	.375*
	Sig. (2-tailed)	.045
	N	29

*. Correlation is significant at the 0.05 level (2-tailed).

Table 16 indicates that there is a significant relation between pupils' performance and the level parental responsibility, however it is a medium and positive correlation (r (29) = .375, p < 0.05). The implication of this findings gives is that the two variables tend to change in the same direction, and again in the context of our investigation, increase in the level of responsible parenting and attitude towards their wards will yield an increase in the performances of the pupils, on the other hand irresponsible parenting and poor parental attitudes will have a corresponding low academic performance of the pupils.

Socio-economic status of parents and their parenting attitudes/responsibilities

Research question six was on finding the statistical relationship between SES of the parents and parenting attitudes/responsibilities. Both variables were transformed into continuous scales; consequently, Pearson Product Moment Correlation Coefficient was used for the analysis. Table 17 contains information on the relationship between two variables.

Table 17

Relation between socio-economic status of parents and parenting attitude

		Parental attitude and responsibility
Socio Economic Status of Parents	Pearson Correlation	.382*
	Sig. (2-tailed)	.041
	N	29

*. Correlation is significant at the 0.05 level (2-tailed).

Table 17 indicates that there is a significant relation between SES of parents and the level of parental attitudes/ responsibilities towards their wards' education, there is however it is a medium and positive correlation ($r(29) = .382$, $p < 0.05$). The implication of this findings gives is that the two variables tend to change in the same direction, and again in the context of our investigation, increase in the level of SES of parents will yield increased parenting and attitude towards their wards on the other hand, low SES of parents may yield a corresponding poor parental attitudes/responsibilities towards their wards.

Gravetter and Forzana (2006) advanced that correlation research study measures two variables to establish the pattern of relationship existing between those two relationships and the strength of their relationship. These kinds of relation are computed in numerical values ranging from -1 to +1 name as Coefficient of correlation. On the same subject, Best (1977) have classified the positive values of Correlation Coefficient (r) as follows; 1) $r = 0.0$ to 0.09 as no relation, 2) $r = .10$ to $.29$ as small/weak, 3) $r = .30$ to $.49$ medium and 4) $r = .50$ to 1.0 large/strong.

So far, the study have revealed that all the three correlation analysis conducted there are relations and the coefficient of correlation values fall within the medium values of the Coefficient of Correlation; Pupils performance and SES of parents($r (29) = .463, p = .011$), Pupils performance and parenting attitude/responsibilities ($r (29) = .375, p = 0.45$), SES of parents and Parental attitude/responsibilities ($r (29) = .382, p = 0.041$).

The result therefore falls in line with various studies and arguments raised on the subject under review by earlier researchers.

Jeynes (2002), did establish that the SES of parents and the extent of their responsible parenting influence the academic performance of their children in the school and in their engagement in extracurricular activities of these as well.

Again, Walters (1998) found out that student performance is very much dependent of SES backgrounds of parents, and Reynolds et al (1993) concluded in their studies that the most constant predictor of children's academic achievement and social adjustment were linked to the expectations of their parents, parents' educational attainment and extent of parental satisfaction with their wards' education at a school.

Again, Davis-Kean (1999) conducted a study on the effect of Socio-economic characteristics on parenting and child outcome, and concluded that responsible parenting plays a significant role in the academic achievement of students. It was further established in that study that Socio-economic factors are directly linked to the academic achievement of school children.

With reference to Table 1, the pupils of Archbishop Porter Primary School – Class two – were found to be just above average students, it was observed on Table 12 that about 86.6% of their parents have SES range of Average to High and scored a parental attitude/responsibility rating of just above average (See Table 14). It can therefore be inferred that the students are not non-performers; that the parents are not irresponsible and finally not extremely poor.

The question then would be that in this scenario could it be inferred that since parental SES and attitudes appeared to be average that is why the pupils are average performers? Prediction is not part of the scope of the study, but it is worth appreciation the point raised by Okafor (2007). He shares a counter view that t SES of parents and their parenting styles are not only the determinants of the performance of pupils. He argues that their equal empirical bases asserting that despite the threat of low SES families having their wards performing poorly in school, others in the same level of SES have recorded remarkable academic success in their academic pursuits. The implication of this statement therefore raises the question of role of the teacher, the teachers' methods of teaching; the child's learning styles, the availability of teaching and learning resources, the cognitive and personality development of the child and a host of factors. Notwithstanding, other empirical studies and this study go assert the fact that the role of parents in the education development is very essential to the way the child would conceptualise the value of education.

In conclusion, it worth reviewing the findings of Henderson (1994) which says that families whose children are doing well in school have some things in common and these include; established family schedules, monitor school activities of their children, parents serve as models to children by attitudes of hard work, self-discipline and learning/capacity development, encourage children and motivate them to progress in school and finally create a conducive family inter- relationship environments for enhanced communication.

CHAPTER FIVE

SUMMARY, CONCLUSION AND RECOMMENDATIONS

Summary

This study is set out to look at the influence of SES of parents and their parental attitude/responsibilities on the academic performance of pupils in the Archbishop Porter 'A' School in Effia Kuma a suburb of Sekondi Takoradi. It also established the academic performance of the pupils, the SES of the parents and the kind of parenting offered to their children.

A descriptive research design type was adopted for the study. Test scores of pupils covering one year's academic results based on the School Based Assessment (SBA) structure was used the establish the academic performance of the pupils and questionnaire were used to obtain information on the SES of the parents and their parental Attitude/responsibilities.

Twenty-nine pupils who are in Basic two having an average age of seven years participated in the study. Questionnaire and test were used as instrument for data collection. The items on the questionnaire measuring the SES of parents and their parenting attitude/responsibilities and the test items measuring the academic performance of the pupils were tested for internal consistency using Cronbach's Alpha Coefficient. The results were, 39 item questionnaire ($\alpha = .91$) and the 18 test results ($\alpha = .94$).

The findings of the study per the data gathered and analysed are as follows;

1. Most of the two class pupils of Archbishop Porter primary school have an academic performance just above average (M = 2.5, SD = 1.2) implying that academically they are not performing poorly.

2. Most (86.2%) of the parents of the pupils have SES level ranging from Average to High SES.

3. Level of parenting attitude in terms of responsible parenting was just above average (M = 2.1, SD = .71).

4. Statistically, there is a significant positive medium correlation between the SES of parents and the academic performance of pupils (r (29) = .463, p < .05).

5. There is a significant positive medium correlation between pupils' performance and the attitude of the parents towards the education of the pupils ((r (29) = .375, p < .05).

6. Parents' SES and their Parenting attitude/responsibilities are statistically related with a positive medium correlate on. (r (29) = .382, p < .05).

Conclusions

It was the intent of the investigator to relate home conditions of pupils in Archbishop Porter 'A' Primary school and their academic. The findings indicated a general medium relation between pupils' academic performance and home conditions which were based on the SES of parents and Parenting attitude/responsibilities.

Children all over the world do have the right to be educated; consequently the school is tasked to play such role in the society. This role cannot be done without the support of parents and guardians of the beneficiaries of education.

This study have brought to the fore that children need parental support to accomplish many things in their lives. As advanced by Walberg (1984) he asserts that an academically stimulated home is a key determinant of learning behaviours of students.

The study has appropriately provided answers to questions raised about the academic performance of pupils, the SES of their parents and the kind of parenting attitudes and responsibilities exhibited by their parents.

Even though, teachers had different view of the pupils in the school the findings of the study portrays a different the above picture. My opinion on the results is that it have offered deeper understanding on the problem identifies and further gives a subtle impression that the parental lapses appears to be filled by the Government's educational interventions namely, free tuition, supply of free exercise books and the school feeding project.

Teachers in the school therefore have to start assessing their own performances and their philosophies regarding their professional practices. This can be done in relation to how they see their pupils. In this context the pupils in the school would be properly understood and appropriately handled for their overall and total development. The entire study had been a worthwhile exercise and has achieved the objectives it set out to accomplish.

Recommendations

Based on the findings of the study, the following recommendations are advanced;

1. School based in-service training for teacher capacity development should be intensified, so as to sharpen the professional conduct of the teachers.
2. School authorities as a matter of policy undertake projects and activities that will attract parents of the pupils to visit the school.
3. Teachers in the school should adopt a strategy of conducting one – on – one interview with their pupils in order to appreciate their challenges at school and at home and according inform their parents.

Suggestions for further studies

As a follow up to this study it is suggested that;

1. A research be carried out on the influence teacher use of instructional hours on the academic performance of pupils in the Archbishop Porter 'A' School.

REFERENCES

Ainley, J., Brian, G., Long, M. & Magaret, B. (1995). Socio-economic status and school education. Canberra: DEET/ACER

Baharudin, R. & Luster, T. (1998). Factors related to the quality of home environment and children's achievement. *Journal of Family Issues* 19(4), 375 – 403.

Barry, J. (2005). *The effect of socio-economic status on academic achievement.* Unpublished dissertation, Wichita State University.

Battle, J. & Lewis, M. (2002). The increasing significance of class: The relative effects of race and socioeconomic satus on academic achievement. *Journal of Poverty*, 6(2), 21 – 35.

Considine, & Zappala, G.(2002). Factors influencing the educational performace of students from disadvantaged backgrounds. In Eardley, T. & Bradbury, B.(Eds), *Competing visions: Refereed proceedings of the National Social Policy Conference* 2001, SPRC Report 1/02. Sydney: University of New South Wales.

Crosnoe, R., Johnson, M.K. & Elder Jr. (2004). School size and the interpersonal side of education: An examination of race/ethnicity and organisational context. *Social Science Quarterly*, 85(5), 1259-1274.

Davis-Kean, P.E.(1999). *The effect of socio economic characteristics on parenting and child outcomes*. Paper presented at biennal meeting society for research in child development. Albuquerque, New Mexico, April 1999.

Eamon, M.K., (2005). Social demographic, school, neighbourhood and parenting influences on academic achievement of Latino young adolescents. *Journal of Youth and Adolescence,* 34(2), 163-175.

Hanafi, Z. (2008), The relationship between aspects of socio-economic factors and academic achievement. *Jurnal Pendidikan* 33(2008) p. 95-105.

Henderson, A. & Berla, A. (1994). A new generation of evidence: The family is critical to student achievement. San Diego: San Diego County Office of Education.

Hijazi, S.T. & Naqvi, S.M.M.R.(2006). Factors affecting students performance. *Bangledesh e-Journal of Sociology. Volume* 3, Number 1. January 2006.

Jeynes, W.H. (2002). Examining the effects of parental absence on the academic achievements of adolescents: The challenge of controlling the family income. *Journal of Family and Economic Issues* (Electronic Version).

Majoribanks, K. (1996). Family learning environments and students outcome: A Review. *Journal of Comparative Family Studies*, 27(2), 373-394.

Mankoe (2001). Methods and Materials for primary school teaching 1. Winneba: IEDE - University of Education.

Okafor, P.C. (2007). Factors contributing to the academic achievement of low socio-economic status students in Anambra South County, Anambra State, Nigeria. Unpublished doctoral theses, St. Jonh's University, Jamaica.

Reynolds, A.J., Nancy, A.M., Hageman, M. & Bezruczko, N.(1993). Schools, families and children: Sixth year results from longitudinal study of children at risk. Chicago: Chicago Public Schools, Department of Research, Evaluation and Planning.

Walberg, H.J. (February 1984). "Families as partners in educational productivity". *Phi Delta Kapan 65*.

APPENDIX A

UNIVERSITY OF EDUCATION, WINNEBA
INSTITUTE OF EDUCATIONAL DEVELOPMENT AND EXTENSION
CAPE COAST CENTRE

Dear Parent,

In an attempt to improve teaching and learning in the Archbishop Porter A1 School you and your ward/child have been selected to be part of a research activity in the Effia Kuma – circuit. Please respond to the questions/indicators posed below by ticking (√) the answers that best fits you; you may also let someone write the answers for you as you tell him/her the responses. You will be required to respond to enquiries on

- Your parenting practices,
- Your Social Economic Status

Be assured that information provided will be treated be treated as highly confidential and will not be related to you in person and would be use exclusively this research. In line with this promise you are advised not to write your name.

Thank you for the cooperation.

Please **tick** (√) the appropriate box to show how often you do the activity indicated under the parenting attitude column.

PART A – PARENTING PRACTICES

S/No	Parenting Attitudes/Styles	Responses		
		Not at all	Sometimes	Always
1	I attend PTA meetings.			
2	I visit my child at his/her school to check his/her regularity and punctuality at school.			
3	I visit my child's school to observe his work/exercises.			
4	I inspect the home work my child brings from school.			
5	I assist my child to ensure home work is done.			
6	I read my child's end of term assessment report (Report Card).			
7	I interview and counsel child about school life.			
8	I attend funfair and merry making occasions with my child. (E.g. Beach, Party etc).			
9	I attend church/mosque/religious ceremonies with child.			
10	I accompany my child to school.			
11	I ensure that my child studies after school before he/she goes to sleep.			

PART B : SOCIO-ECONOMIC STATUS OF PARENTS

Please **tick** (√) the appropriate box that best fits into your living standards. Be assured that this information would be kept confidential and would be used only for this research. Again, the analysis and discussions regarding this information will not be linked to you personally.

Thank you.

1. What is the highest level of qualification of one of your parents/guardian?
   - [ ] Elementary School/Primary
   - [ ] JHS/Middle School
   - [ ] Vocational Training
   - [ ] SHS/Technical Institute
   - [ ] Diploma/Polytechnic
   - [ ] University/Degree
   - [ ] Postgraduate

2. Which of the following statements apply to you in terms of the occupational status of one of your parents?
   - [ ] Not Working at the moment
   - [ ] Casual or Part time work
   - [ ] Engaged in Full time work
   - [ ] Run his/her own business

3. What is the position of the bread winner in his/her work
   - [ ] Labourer
   - [ ] Skilled / Artisan
   - [ ] Headman/Forman
   - [ ] Supervisor
   - [ ] Manager/Director

4. How much income comes to the house at the end of the month
   - [ ] Less than GHc 50.00
   - [ ] Between GHc 50.00 - GHc 150.00
   - [ ] Between GHc 150.00 - GHc 500.00
   - [ ] Between 500 .00 -GHc1000
   - [ ] Over GHc 1000

5. Do you have a car in the house?
   - [ ] No
   - [ ] Yes

6. Do you have Television in your house?

- [ ] No
- [ ] Yes

7. Do you have a fridge in your house?
   - [ ] No
   - [ ] Yes

8. Do your parents hold any Religious positions?
   - [ ] No
   - [ ] Yes

9. Is the family able to have three meals a day?
   - [ ] No
   - [ ] Yes

10. Apart from your parents has any family member completed university education?
    - [ ] No
    - [ ] Yes